IMAGES OF ENGLAND

GORTON
MONASTERY

IMAGES OF ENGLAND

GORTON
MONASTERY

THE MONASTERY OF
ST FRANCIS AND GORTON TRUST

The
History
Press

Frontispiecee: A Whit walk on Whit Friday, *c*.1960. The friars, led by Father Martin Crawley (guardian 1957-1960), walk behind the banner, together with the girls holding the banner strings. From left to right: Fathers Theodore, Arthur, -?-, -?-, Athanasius, Luke, Bruno and Rudolph process along Gorton Lane near Queen's Road, going towards Church Lane, with the New Inn behind them on Crossley Street.

First published in 2004 by Tempus Publishing
Reprinted 2006

Reprinted in 2009 by
The History Press
The Mill, Brimscombe Port,
Stroud, Gloucestershire, GL5 2QG
www.thehistorypress.co.uk

© The Monastery of St Francis and Gorton Trust, 2009

The right of The Monastery of St Francis and Gorton Trust to be identified as the Author of this work has been asserted in accordance with the Copyrights, Designs and Patents Act 1988.

British Library Cataloguing in Publication Data.
A catalogue record for this book is available from the British Library.

ISBN 978 0 7524 3208 3

Typesetting and origination by
Tempus Publishing Limited.
Printed in Great Britain..

Contents

A Whit Walk on Whit Friday in the 1950s. The banner of St Francis is carried aloft along Gorton Lane, with the page boys of the May Queen leading. Crossley House is in the background on the left. In 1895, 1,300 had taken part in the walk.

Acknowledgements

The members of the team who produced this book are:

Jill Cronin: research and text
Frank Rhodes: research
Graham North: additional photographs and text
Tony Hurley: monastery historian
Marie Koudellas: archivist
David Ratcliffe: scanning photographs

We should like to thank all those who have helped us or kindly allowed use of their photographs in this book: Pauline Bardsley, M. Barratt, family of the late Eileen Bosanko, Audrey Bradshaw, Des and Vera Bromage, Agnes Burns, Margaret and Tony Carroll, Marjorie Cooke, R. Allan Crockford, Helen and Shamus Devlin, Mary Drinkhill, Josie and Peter Faulkner, Austin Fawley, Pat Fernandes, Tony Fitzgerald, Mavis Gasse, Kenneth Goodwin, Revd David Gray, Elaine and Paul Griffiths, Elizabeth Hardicker, Mrs V. Holmes, the late Stan Horritt, Doreen Johnson, Margaret Jones, Edmund Kenna, Brian Logan, Bernadette McCreavey, Mrs M. Mooney, Ann Morrissey, Tommy Mullen, Mrs. Nearey, Nora and James Neil, Kath North, Mildred and Lawrence Quiligotti, Sheila Quinn, Ged Redman, Frank and Laura Rhodes, Bernard Roddy, Ilma Scantlebury, Harry Scarsbrook, Jean Smith, Ursula Smith, Sotheby's Ltd, Irene and Colin Southworth, K. Spiller, Thelma and Kevin Thatcher, Rita and Jim Thomas, K. Walker, Janet Wallwork, and Patricia Wengraf Ltd. We thank all those who have helped in any way.

Introduction

Anyone travelling around East Manchester is aware of the lofty façade of the monastery church of St Francis of Assisi in West Gorton. Passers-by along Gorton Lane, dwarfed by the awesome height and splendour of the derelict church and friary, are left wondering about its past.

In 1872, it 'was the largest parish church built in England since the Reformation' (*From Assisi to Gorton*. Father Agnellus 1938) and it is thought to be the largest single-storey building in Manchester. This Grade II★ listed building towers 98ft from the floor to the ceiling and measures 194ft in length. In the 1940s it was described as 'of cathedral proportions and probably the finest and most beautiful parish church in the North of England'. English Heritage state, 'The church is E.W. Pugin's most ambitious work and towers above the flat landscape of East Manchester, a striking symbol of the Catholic faith in this city'.

How did it come to exist in an industrialised suburb of Manchester, once set amid rows of terraced housing? In 1861, a group of Belgian Franciscan friars said their first mass in the school/chapel in the rural setting of Gorton Lane. They moved into nearby Bankfield Cottage and, between 1863 and 1872, in less than ten years, a three-sided friary with a cloistered garden and adjoining church arose. In spite of setbacks and local hardships during the Depression, funds were raised to add four schools and a Parochial Hall, with beautiful grounds stretching to the Corn Brook. For the Golden Jubilee in 1911, the distinctive 50ft-high church spire was constructed. The parish stretched from Ardwick to Cross Street, Gorton, and from Hyde Road to the canal, growing from 300 parishioners in 1862 to 6,000 in 1901.

The monastery was the centre of social life; 1,300 people walked on Whit Friday in 1895. This book tells their story through beginnings, development and decline, and describes this gem of architecture inside and outside with its onetime wealth of treasured objects. Included is the community who made the monastery what it is: the guardians, friars, altar boys, May Queens, Whit Walks, special events and groups, such as the Greyfriars Players. Those who were baptised, confirmed and married here are also included, as are the four schools.

The Pugin family, too, was important, as was Brother Patrick Dalton, who carried out so much of the construction work. The firm of Pugin, Ashlin & Pugin was employed, with Edward Welby Pugin designing the church and his brother Peter Paul designing most of the altars. They were following in the footsteps of their famous father, Augustus Welby Northmore Pugin, a champion of Gothic architecture in Victorian Britain.

Decline set in with a fall in the number of parishioners, as local terraced housing was cleared in the 1960s and '70s and workplaces were closed down. The formation of the new parish of the Sacred Heart in 1901 also depleted numbers.

The Franciscans had some hard decisions to make. Despite the fundraising efforts of the faithful few, they had to admit that times were changing and that it was time to move on. A property developer was lurking in the wings, anxious to take over this prized Pugin treasure and all its fittings. In November 1989 the last mass was held, the church was deconsecrated and the doors were closed on the concerned Gorton community.

The flats scheme failed and the property developers went bankrupt in the early 1990s and Gorton Monastery was left unprotected and was repeatedly vandalised. Everything that was of value and removable was stripped out. Even the twelve precious 8ft-high sandstone statues of saints spent an embarrassing twelve months in a junk/antique yard in Longsight, before appearing in a Sotheby's catalogue as garden ornaments. Through the diligence of a local resident, Janet Wallwork, the city council and press were alerted and complex negotiations ensued. For the costly sum of £25,000, those precious saints (with damaged limbs and bruises) are now safely in storage, awaiting their return to their rightful home in Gorton.

Paul Griffiths is a former St Francis pupil and altar boy and he and his wife, Elaine, founded The Monastery of St Francis & Gorton Trust, which he now chairs. This charitable trust recruited trustees and an army of volunteers and immediately began work to raise funds and carry out feasibility work on how the buildings could be saved and used in the future. It was important to find a suitable use that would bring benefits to the local community and safeguard the future of this important site.

The site's architectural and spiritual significance was recognised when the monastery was placed on the World Monuments Fund Watch List of the 100 most endangered sites between 1998 and 2001, alongside the Taj Mahal, Pompeii and the Valley of the Kings.

After years of fundraising, surveys, feasibility studies and development work, involving extensive planning and consultation with the local community, partners and stakeholders, the Trust is delighted that a solution was eventually found. An exciting new future for Gorton Monastery lies ahead.

Through the work of the Trust and its volunteers, almost £6.5 million of funding has been raised for the Monastery. Using the £3.66 million grant promised by the Heritage Lottery Fund, £300,000 from English Heritage and £2.2 million of ERDF funds from Europe, work began in late 2005. The restored buildings re-opened in June 2007.

The future plans for the Monastery are unique, combining cultural heritage and exhibitions with a conference, training and enterprise centre. In the former church, the High Altar and Private Chapel will be restored, providing a Holy Centre to the site, recreating a spiritual sanctuary and providing a place for weddings, christenings and family occasions again.

This important landmark has become the focal point of the area again, which will also generate new business enterprises, training, exhibitions, events and social, educational and health facilities. All these will contribute significantly to the local economy and quality of life of its local residents.Let Sir Nikolaus Pevsner (*South Lancashire, The Buildings of England series*) have the last words on what he calls a church of national importance. 'It is meant to be a demonstration, and it has remained a showpiece.'

Jill Cronin and Elaine Griffiths

Due to popular demand, this is now the third reprint of *Gorton Monastery* which has been extended, compiled and updated by Graham North, the Monastery's resident photographer. The Monastery story has a very happy ending and we are thrilled to see the buildings lovingly restored and in regular use for a very wide range of activities. Our modern Monastery is operated by our own social enterprise trading company, The Monastery Manchester, providing high quality special events, conferences, meetings, tours, weddings, concerts, health and well-being, spiritual and cultural events. All the proceeds generated through the use of the buildings are donated to the Trust to help with the ongoing conservation and maintenance. The Trust continues to fundraise to complete the work and restoration, and to continue delivering charitable, educational and cultural projects for the community.

The Monastery is open to the public every Sunday from 12.00 a.m. until 4.00 p.m. and a full list of all our events and activities can be found on our website: www.themonastery.co.uk

Thank you for your support and we look forward to welcoming you to the Monastery soon.

Elaine Griffiths, MBE
Chief Executive
September 2009

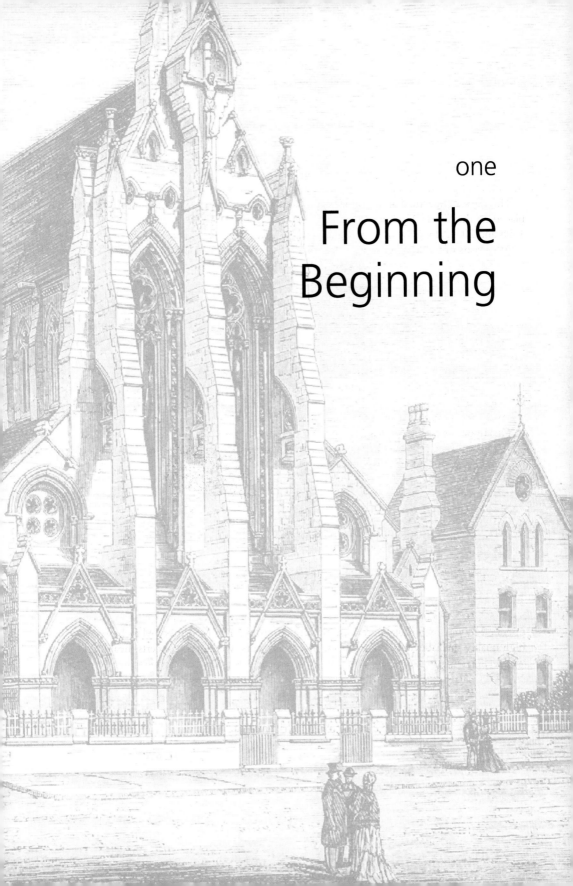

one

From the Beginning

The first Franciscan friars in Gorton in 1861. From left to right, back row: Fathers Francis Verhagen, Germain Verleyen. Middle row: Fathers Archangel Vendrickx, Emmanuel Kenners, Patrick Verherstraeten. Front row: Fathers Bruno de Grave, Willibrord van den Neucker. They were sent by the Belgian Province in 1858 to Sclerder in Cornwall. In 1861, with the Bishop of Salford's permission, they took over the existing mission at St Anne in Fairfield, Manchester. Father Emmanuel was the first Superior until 1862, when Father Francis became the first guardian at Gorton.

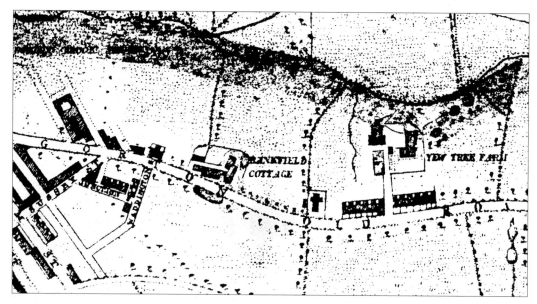

A map of West Gorton, showing Bankfield Cottage with the school/chapel to the right, 1863. Father Peter Cardinael of Fairfield was just completing this school/chapel on Gorton Lane. The friars held their first mass here on Christmas Day in 1861. Bankfield Cottage, a large nearby house with around 4 acres, was purchased as a friary, from gifts of £2,000 from fathers of the Second Province who had retired to Taunton convent, and £500 from a benefactor, Thomas Luck. On 25 April 1862 the friars moved in.

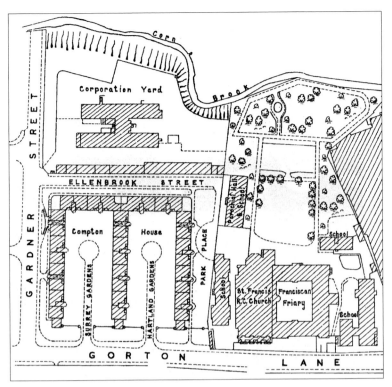

A plan of the final layout and size of the monastery complex, 1957. Where fields such as Bank Field, Barn Meadow, Old Croft and Yarn Croft had stood alongside Yew Tree Farm, the monastery was to take shape. Its church stood on the site of Bankfield Cottage, the friary stretched out beside it towards the first school/chapel and the gardens spread northwards to the Corn Brook.

The interior of the school/chapel in the late 1800s. In 1932, Mr T.A. Butterworth of Leeds wrote to the friars, describing the school as it was seventy years previously, in 1862/3, 'The school was divided in the centre with moveable pictures making two compartments of it, and Miss Marr's desk was taken away at the weekends for mass on Sunday...we took our dinners and dined on the banks of the small brook [Corn Brook], which ran behind the school at this time'.

Left: Pugin's design for the monastery church and friary. The firm of Messrs Pugin, Ashlin & Pugin was engaged, with Edward Welby Pugin as architect. Aged only twenty-four, he had already been employed to carry out work by Father Emmanuel Kenners at Sclerder in Cornwall in 1858.

Below left: a bust of Edward Welby Pugin (1834-1875) in Ramsgate. As the eldest son of the famous architect, Augustus Pugin, and his first wife who died in childbirth, he became head of the family firm when his father died in 1852. His brother, Paul, designed some of the altars in the monastery church. Ashlin was his brother-in-law.

Opposite above left: The friars in the beginnings of their new church in the late 1860s. To the right would be the High altar and behind them the confessionals on the west side of the church. The first stone of the first wing of the friary was laid by Canon Benoit on Whit Sunday, May 1863 and the friary was completed by 1867. The lofty church which was built last, with its first stone laid in June 1866, was opened on 26 September 1872, having taken just six years to complete.

Opposite above right: The friars outside their new friary on Gorton Lane, 1867. This copper negative plate is one of a pair and the other shows the interior of the new church, looking towards the High altar. The first wing of the friary, parallel with the later girls' school, was opened on the Feast of St Francis 1863, by Bishop Turner. The friars had to continue living in Bankfield Cottage, as that wing, where later the refectory and library would be, had to serve as the church, since the school was overflowing in the school/chapel.

Father Cuthbert Wood as vicar blessed
the church and designed the statues
and some windows (see p.116). Fathers
Francis and Germain (see p.10), the
original guardians, oversaw the early
work but building virtually ceased,
as the Fenian Arch incident and
the Murphy Riots caused dislike of
Catholics and support dried up. On
1 May 1871, Father Willibrord (see
p.10) was appointed as guardian with
Father Cuthbert as vicar. They secured
funds, even holding a huge bazaar, and
work restarted. Father Willibrord also
set up a Memorial Register or Golden
Book of benefactors' names (see p.33).

Brother Patrick Dalton, from County Limerick in Ireland, joined the friars at Fairfield, becoming clerk of works. He led scores of local volunteers in demolishing Bankfield Cottage, making bricks, constructing the church and friary and carving the altars. In his crusade for bricks, he scoured all of Manchester, becoming a well-known figure and saving the project pounds. At the opening dinner, Edward Welby Pugin described him 'not as clerk of works (and this he had been magnificently) but as joint architect'.

Father Polycarp Vervoort (guardian 1874-1877 and 1880-1883). With a parish of 4,000 and with eight friars, he continued the work of the guardian Father Francis, who had erected a new infants' school in 1866, by providing a separate girls' school in 1874. Rector of the Seraphic College at Gorton, which trained new friars from 1881 to 1895, until its removal to Buckingham, he died in office in 1896. He was 'a very great priest, born in 1826 in Belgium,...ordained in 1849....and truly one of the Franciscan pioneers, who built up the Church and parish in Gorton and the Order in England.'

Father Richard O'Connor (guardian 1896-1898). As Hugh O'Connor, he was one of the first boys to pass through the Seraphic College in 1885. At the New Year party in the infants' school in 1897, he expressed a need for a parish hall. In spite of local poverty because of the engineers' strike, he was supported enthusiastically in fundraising and the Parochial Hall was founded that same year by Bishop Bilsborrow, who also opened it in 1899. Brother Patrick Dalton oversaw its construction, supported by Father Peter Hickey (guardian 1899-1902).

The Parochial Hall on the edge of the monastery garden, *c*.1912. St Francis's Hall cost about £2,000 and became the centre of parish life. It hosted parties, the Easter Soirée (begun by Father Aidan in 1884), concerts, guild and fraternity meetings, sodalities, the choir, the Greyfriars Players, socials, dances, lectures, demonstrations, meetings and the Youth Club. One of its first uses was for a bazaar, one of many to raise vast funds. The ground floor housed the parish library and kitchen and on the first floor was a hall.

The Gorton friars at their Tertiary Congress, June 1921. They did much for the Third Order in the north, where laymen followed the Franciscan ideals in their daily life. This congress, organised by Father Agnellus, was supported wholeheartedly by the Tertiary Bishop, Louis Casartelli. At the congress of 1938, Bishop Henshaw was himself received into the Third Order. Catholics came to Gorton from Stockport, Runcorn and Rochdale to join this Order.

The community at Gorton in the late 1930s. From left to right, back row: Brothers Anthony and Kenneth, Fathers Camillus, Agnellus, Stanislaus and Giles, Brothers Conrad and James. Front row: Fathers Augustine, Robert, Harold Richardson (guardian 1936–1939), Roger, Albert. The church was consecrated on 22 June 1938 by the Bishop, Dr Henshaw.

George Beck, Bishop of Salford, unveiling the foundation stone of the new secondary school in the monastery grounds on Saturday 21 July 1956. The bishop gave the Pontifical Blessing on the school. On his left is Father Theodore (see pp.51 and 109) and clapping just behind him is Leslie Lever. Altar boys stand on the left. The guardian at that time was Father Walter Hobson (1954-1957) (see p.50).

Flash the dog tries to join the ceremony at the laying of the foundation stone of the school on 21 July 1956 (see p.92). Leslie Lever MP is amused, and attempts to continue his speech while a gentleman tries to tempt Flash away. The spectators clearly enjoyed the impromptu show. Afterwards they filed past the foundation stone, while the monastery band played (see p.98). Teas were then served in the Parochial Hall.

Sister Thomas Moore, Jean Roddy, stands outside the front doors of the monastery church on the occasion of the centenary celebrations in 1961. Jean's brother, Bernard, was head altar boy (see pp.52-53). Kathleen Mulheran (see p.106) watches by the column. To celebrate the Golden Jubilee in 1911, there was a four day bazaar with a souvenir booklet and Bishop Casartelli presided at the services. Father Athanasius Johnstone (guardian 1910-1911) suggested that the spire be erected on the front of the church and it was in place by December 1911 (see p.25).

Father Ronald, the last guardian, is praying at the steps of the sanctuary in front of the High altar. Funding in 1980 helped to re-roof the church and carry out some exterior repairs, but the front wing of the friary had to be demolished in the 1970s for safety reasons. Falling numbers due to house clearances and closure of local workplaces, plus an ageing, dwindling community of friars, led to their removal from Gorton, after the last mass on 26 November 1989.

two

An Outside Tour

The monastery church and Gorton Lane, from outside All Saints' church on Queen's Road in the early 1950s. The four main portals screened by a porch, itself entered under four moulded and gabled archways, run the width of the church. The turning into Neill Street is on the right, with a newsagent on its corner and then the turning into Laurence Street. Queen's Road bends to the right with near left Light and then Ashbourne Streets.

Almost the full frontage of the monastery complex along Gorton Lane, viewed from the south-east, with the church on the left, friary centre and the girls' school on the right, 1966. The boys' school is to the right and the infants' school lies on the left between the church and Brook House flats. Once railings graced the front wall but they were removed for the war effort.

Opposite above: Gorton Lane looking eastwards, *c.*1915. Nowadays the monastery complex stands isolated, near modern housing. Until house clearances took place in the 1970s, it was surrounded by rows of terraced housing and Gorton Lane was lined with shops. On the left are Grantham and Gardner Streets, later Park Place and Hartland Gardens. Opposite the church stands 'the Holy Row', where people connected with the monastery, such as the cleaners, lived.

Opposite below: A painting of the monastery by the architect, Edward Welby Pugin. The frontage of the church and friary has a wide lawn and a row of trees. A letter from T.A. Butterworth in 1932 describes Gorton Lane in 1862 as 'an avenue of trees. Beside it was a small pond in which a few ducks were disporting themselves, as we passed the residence of the Fathers. Opposite the school was Warburton Farm.'

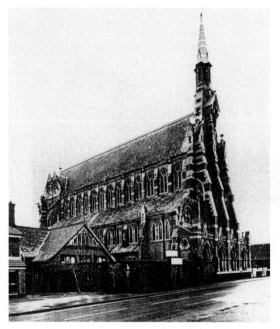

The monastery church and schools, from the south-west on Gorton Lane, 1991. The belfry tower with its copper roof was added in 1911 to celebrate the Golden Jubilee, on the suggestion of Father Athanasius Johnstone. The church roof survived an incendiary bomb in the Blitz of 1940, as the bomb spent itself out in the guttering. The whole emphasis is vertical.

The back of the monastery church from the north-west, 1991. On the right is the back of the infants' school and on the left the private friary chapel juts out from the friary wall. The Parochial Hall and the gardens have gone, except for the enclosed garden within the cloisters. Modern housing backs onto the site. Topping the roof is the cross with its corona.

The site viewed from the north-east, 1991. The church is in the background and two sides of the friary are visible, plus the private friary chapel jutting out on the right. Gorton Lane runs in front on the left side. This open area once housed the girls' and boys' schools and the original school/chapel.

The Parochial Hall north of the church, 1991, (see p.15). By the early 1970s this building had gone: modern housing now lies on its site and on Park Place, which lay alongside it. Beyond the hall the vegetable garden of the friars once lay, along with the tennis courts, where the senior school would later be built (see pp.17 and 92). The monastery grounds stretched right up to the Corn Brook on the north side of the site.

The bell-cote on the friary roof with the church wall on the right. The cross on the bell-cote roof is echoed by the cross and corona on the church roof, just hidden by the chimney on the right. The cross on the roof of the church is set in a corona near the junction of the friary and church walls. Surrounded by a crown of thorns that show Christ's victory over death, it rises from the corona. The rose-shaped windows of the church and the details of the architecture are seen here close-up. They include the polychromatic bands of local red bricks, Derbyshire sandstone dressings and blue black bricks and the gargoyle at the foot of the church roof. The roof was built with Welsh slate and was completed in 1872 by the firm of W. Southern at a cost of £1,925.

The statue of Our Lady on the east side of the church, 1991. Originally this stood in the entrance of the friary, on the left hand side opposite a fireplace. Mary wears a crown of her own flowers, roses, and underfoot she crushes the serpent of evil.

Above: The front façade of the church.
High up stands the statue of Our Lord,
Christ Crucified. At the feet of Our Lord
stand statues of Our Lady on the left and
of John the Evangelist on the right, each
on a small column. The spire was described
at the time as the 'finest and highest in
England'.

Right: Our Lord, Christ Crucified. Above
him are the letters INRI, which stand for,
'Iesus Nazarenus Rex Iudaeorum' (John
19.19) and translate from Latin as, 'Jesus
of Nazarus, King of the Jews'. Around the
figures, the stonework is carved in great
detail with plants, mouldings and other
decoration and the view over Gorton is
breathtaking.

The friary garden, enclosed by the cloisters, with the church on the left and the rear wall of the friary in the background. Once it was lovingly cared for by the friars and their gardener (in 1881 Bryan Maguire) and by Father Anselm Keane (guardian 1918-1921), who was devoted to the beauty of these grounds. He planted three hundred trees and grassed the lawns. The friars handed this garden over to clergy on retreat and to gatherings for outdoor processions.

Another view of the friary garden, flanked by the walls of the cloisters. Each cloister is 100ft long and Gothic in style but with a plain interior with arches and a simple tiled floor scheme (see p.117). The front cloister was knocked down, together with the front wing of the friary, in the 1970s. A door at the rear of the garden gives onto the cloisters and so into the friary (see p.118) or into the church by a door at the south-east corner of the nave.

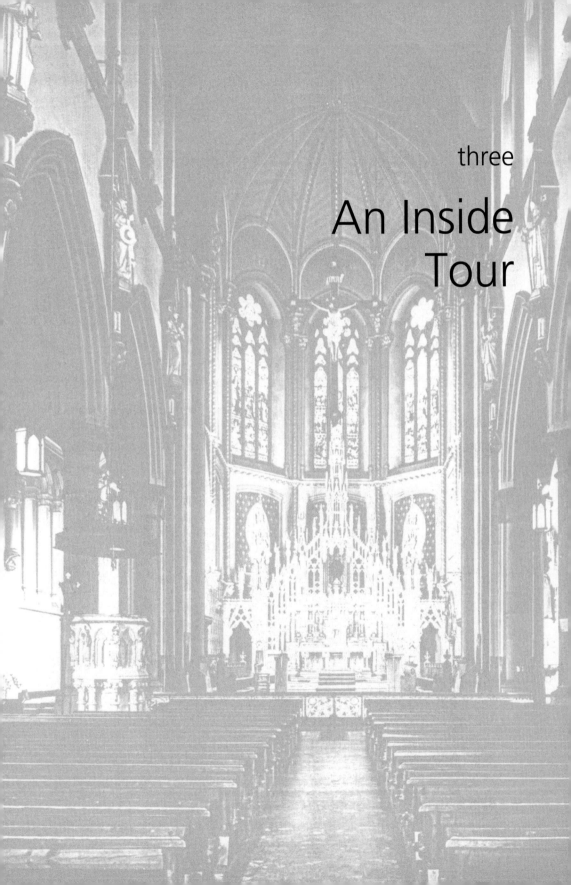

three

An Inside
Tour

The mosaic with the badge of the Franciscans, on the floor of the monastery church in the nave, just within the front entrance. The Latin words translate as 'My God and my all'. The mosaic was cleaned for the centenary in 1961, on the instruction of Father Martin Crawley (guardian 1957-1960). Here the stigmata appear on the hand of St Francis and on that of Christ.

The nave of the church, from the High altar, 1966. This rare view shows the layout of the oak benches, placed in the nave and aisles in 1876. Above the entrance is the organ loft and choir gallery. The organ, built by Wadsworth of Manchester to mark the end of the first guardianship of Father Aidan McCarthy (1883-1886), was funded by a three-day bazaar and was opened in July 1888, with Father Augustine d'Hooge from Glasgow as organist. Later, when it was rebuilt and electrified in 1938, it was blessed by Bishop Thomas Henshaw to mark the seventy-five-year jubilee and was played by T. Sharples, organist for over fifty years.

The sanctuary and nave from the back, 1966. The High altar, which is here lit, dominates the building. In 1885 the guardian Father Aidan McCarthy had the church extended from 184ft to 194ft by this sanctuary, with its High altar and stained-glass windows. The nave is 98ft high and has thirteen bays, with two side aisles, east and west, plus a central aisle. The pulpit stands to the left of the sanctuary (see p.36). The reredos behind the altar, made of marble and alabaster with flying buttresses supporting a great central canopy over 40ft high, was one of the highest in the country.

The nave and sanctuary in the 1940s. The nave is empty of pews, perhaps because the floor was being repaired. In 1876 dry rot was discovered in the wooden floor and had to be removed. In 1882 tiling of Irish limestone replaced it, resting on brickwork to allow the circulation of air. The elaborate tiling in the central aisle was described as being 'like a carpet'. The floor was retiled in 1961 for the centenary.

A rare and puzzling view of the sanctuary at Christmas. The sanctuary and side aisle are viewed through a screen, which bears the Latin inscription, 'Glory to God in the Highest'. It seems to be a special decoration for Christmas. The sanctuary has two bays, a polygonal apse and columns of red Mansfield stone. The effect is thirteenth-century Gothic and, as Edward died in 1875, his brother Peter Paul Pugin designed the High altar. Brother Patrick Dalton executed the work in his workshop on the north side of the garden. It was consecrated by Bishop Ilsley of Birmingham on 5 July 1885. The Communion altar rails of wrought iron were donated by Mrs Scaife and the corona and sanctuary lamp by Mr Fopato. Stencilling covers the sanctuary walls and the left wall beneath the window.

Above: The decorated ceiling of the sanctuary, 2002. This lofty ceiling escaped the hands of the looters and still boasts its groined decoration. Angels, stencilled on the wall, decorate the small area between the ceiling and each window.

Right: The crucifix, which hung in the sanctuary arch. The Pugins were advocates of returning to Gothic principles and so this crucifix was suspended in front of the High altar, where the rood screen used to be in churches (see pp 29-30). Each corner of the cross bears an evangelist, the bottom one being St Matthew, and above is the inscription 'INRI' (see p.25). The massive, polychromed, stone cross (17ft/526cm) was located at a London art dealer, Pat Wengraf Ltd. Pat kindly agreed to let the Trust purchase the crucifix for the same amount she had paid for it. The crucifix finally returned to its rightful place on 2 November 2006.

The stained-glass window in the wall of the polygonal apse of the sanctuary on the left-hand side. This is one of three and depicts St Clare, St Bonaventure and St Louis King of France. The right window depicts St Elizabeth of Hungary, St Louis Bishop and St Colette. The centre window depicts the life and acts of St Francis. So the three orders instituted by St Francis are each represented in the sanctuary. Designed by G. Johnson and made by Edmundson & Son of Manchester in January 1872, they were provided by Father George Dunn, the priest at Hexham.

Details of angels in the bottom of the right hand stained-glass window. Each side window carries these angels with the banner 'Adoro te devote'. All three windows have a rose window and five trefoil lights above. The centre rose window depicts St George. The five central trefoil lights carry the arms of the Order of St Francis and emblematic figures of Poverty, Chastity, Humility and Obedience.

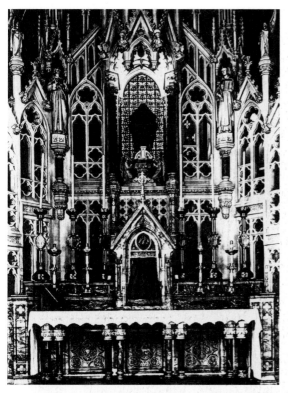

Left: The intricate detail on the High altar. A red and gold lattice work decoration backs the crucifix, which is here covered up for Lent. Behind, canopied niches in the reredos carry the figures of Sts Anthony, Clare, Elizabeth of Hungary and Bonaventure. Three stone steps approach the altar, with its white marble top and alabaster tabernacle, richly carved and moulded with a door of beaten brass. Underneath was housed the Golden Book, recording the names of benefactors. On the altar front are panels carved with emblems of the Eucharist.

Below: The archangel Michael in a stencilled panel, on the left side of the High altar. Originally on the walls behind the altar was a stencilled, decorative pattern, but later they were each filled with a figure of an archangel. In the sanctuary, from left to right: Michael (the defender), Raphael (the healer) and Gabriel (the messenger).

The two stencilled panels on the left of the High altar are pictured. The winged archangel, Raphael, is depicted beneath the stained-glass window. Beneath him the steps wind up to where a dedication on the wall records, 'Pray for the good estate of Mr James McGuirk, through whose munificence this altar was commenced and for all other benefactors'. This altar, which was once one of the largest in the country, was described as 'one of the finest in England'.

The Lady chapel to the left of the sanctuary at the north end of the west nave aisle, 1991. A piscina lies to the right of it. A fund was launched to cover the construction cost of £316 and, among the principal donors, were the Miss Carrolls of Gorton Lane. This altar was also designed by Peter Paul Pugin and the chapel was opened on 13 December 1891.

There is an arched, traceried window above the sanctuary, looking into the upstairs community choir room. This window separates the private chapel from the sanctuary and carries three trefoil-shaped and many rose-shaped lights. Angels support the base of the piers and the walls are stencilled with archangels in gold panels. On the right is the winged archangel Gabriel, with the wall stencilled in red with gold fleurs-de-lys.

The Lady Chapel with banners to Our Lady, in the 1940s. The altar was carved by Richard Lockwood Boulton of Cheltenham and the panels were painted by Hardman's of Birmingham. The window in the chapel was the gift of Mr G. Knightly and was designed by Father Cuthbert Wood (see p.13). The artist was Mr Casilani of St Helen's and it was made by Williams & Wilson of Manchester.

The altar to the Blessed John Forest (priest and martyr 1538), in the north-west corner of the west aisle of the nave, near the altar of Our Lady. The pulpit on the left, built by Jones & Willis and at a cost of £202 5s, in memory of Mrs Dunkerley of Blackley and her mother, was erected by the guardian, Father Aidan McCarthy. It was placed first on the Epistle (right) side of the church but moved to the Gospel (left) side by Brother Patrick in 1883, who also raised it, enlarged the sounding board and added another handrail.

The altar to the Blessed John Forest, with the steps to the pulpit on the left. Of the five altars in the church, this was the last to be built and was funded by Richard Holden of Blackburn, in memory of his wife. He was a benefactor and Syndic of the friary, a devoted member of the Third Order and a Knight of St Gregory. The intricate carvings and figures have sadly all been looted and only a fragment of this altar remains today.

The stencilled paintings above the sanctuary arch facing the nave. The scene depicts Christ in Majesty accompanied by two angels. Below, the top of the tall reredos of the High altar, itself 40ft high, is just visible below the stained glass windows of the sanctuary.

The east side aisle of the nave, looking towards the altars. Straight ahead lies the altar of St Anthony of Padua (priest and theologian), with that of the Sacred Heart at right angles to it. The first statue on the right is of St Joseph holding a lily and the second of St Francis, which is a rare view of the statue in this position, as it usually was sited opposite, on the far wall by the confessionals (see pp.39-41). Along the wall are some of the fourteen Stations of the Cross, all still missing.

The altar to St Anthony of Padua with the vestry door to the boys' sacristy on the right, in the 1940s. The altar, designed by Peter Paul Pugin, was carved by Richard Lockwood Boulton of Cheltenham in 1890/1. Made of alabaster and marble, it was funded principally with £150 by Miss Butti of Taunton, the sister of Thomas Butti (Fatther Brendan Butti at St Francis). They knew Father Aidan when he assisted at Taunton. On the left is a statue of St Joseph with the infant Christ.

The west side-aisle of the nave, looking towards the back and the main entrance. Ahead is the choir loft with the baptistery fronted by the statue of the Pietà below (see p.43). The organ is just visible between the left hand columns. On the right is the statue of St Francis, which was once sited on the opposite, east wall (see p.37). Behind St Francis are the doors to the confessionals with the Stations of the Cross hung above.

The statue of St Francis with a sheep at his feet, with the doors to the confessionals behind. Above hang two of the huge oil paintings of the Stations of the Cross. They were each 4ft high and are now lost. There are six confessionals, but they have twelve doorways. They consist of rooms with two doors each: one entrance for the person making confession and another for the person next in turn. The actual boxes were made of oak.

The altar to the Sacred Heart in the east aisle, to the right of the sacristy door. Completed in 1893 at a cost of £255, the altar was donated by Philip Ross in memory of his father, Edward Ross of Marple, secretary of the Manchester, Sheffield & Lincoln railway works in Gorton. The ornaments on the altar were paid for by the Apostleship of Prayer and the candles form a heart shape. The bell above the door was sent from Belgium by Father James Anselm Millward, having been in the old Franciscan Mission in Abergavenny and reputedly dating from pre-Reformation times.

The west aisle, from the central aisle of the nave, 1968. On the right is the pulpit and in the background are the confessionals, the statue of St Francis, the altar of the Blessed John Forest and several of the Stations of the Cross. Above the pillars are some of the statues of the Franciscan saints with angels at their feet. From left to right: St Louis of France (patron of the Third Order), St Bernadine of Siena, St Bonaventure, St Anthony of Padua.

Some of the saints *in situ*, 1991. St Bonaventure (cardinal and theologian) is on the left and St Anthony of Padua on the right. They have angels at their feet, who are holding the emblem of that saint. The graceful canopies above their heads run into and form part of a string mould, carved with plant life, below the clerestory windows. The High altar and sanctuary are off to the right. The columns are made of Halifax stone, the carvings of Bath stone and the statues of sandstone.

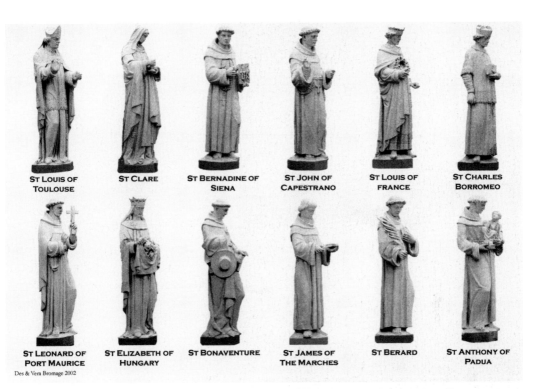

St Louis of Toulouse

St Clare

St Bernadine of Siena

St John of Capestrano

St Louis of France

St Charles Borromeo

St Leonard of Port Maurice

St Elizabeth of Hungary

St Bonaventure

St James of The Marches

St Berard

St Anthony of Padua

Des & Vera Bromage 2002

Above: Statues of the twelve Franciscan saints of the Order of Friars Minor, which stood on pedestals between the arches of the central aisle of the nave. These 6ft-high, life-size figures are made of sandstone. Father Cuthbert Wood (see p.13) designed them and their emblems and they were made by Williams & Wilson of Manchester. The emblems which they carry are special to each saint. Their fate is described on pp.116-117.

Right: The angels each carry an emblem of the Franciscan saint they rest beneath, between the arches on both sides of the central aisle of the nave. A scheme has been set up to 'Save a Saint and Adopt an Angel'.

'Adopt an Angel' MONASTERY TRUST 'Adopt an Angel'

Above: The east aisle of the nave, from the High altar. This has no confessionals on it. At the far right end is the door leading out to the cloisters and up to the choir loft above. The nave has thirteen bays on each side with six arches dividing the aisles. The windows are arcaded three-lights, 18ft above floor level to help light the sanctuary.

Left: The Calvary, near the front doors, at the south end of the east aisle, below the choir loft. Benefactor Richard Holden, Syndic of the friary, gifted this in memory of his wife. On the left is Our Lady and on the right, St John the Evangelist, with Mary Magdalen kneeling. Behind, on wooden boards, are the names of the dead in both world wars. On the left is the doorway to the choir loft and cloisters, beyond which is a sign reading 'Enclosure: no girls allowed'. A statue of St Anthony with the child Jesus, is on the left.

The Pietà of Christ and Mary, which stood in front of the wooden rails of the baptistery, near the front doors, at the south end of the west aisle. The inscription reads, 'O all ye who pass by the way, attend and see if there be any sorrow like to my sorrow.' The font, behind the railings, was made by Brother Patrick Dalton from Irish limestone and was inaugurated on 5 November 1882. He enclosed it with these ornamental wooden rails. Sadly, newspaper archives show The Pietà broken into pieces on the nave floor.

This is the refectory in the friary. The interior of the three-storey friary was simple and unadorned, but very functional. There was a reception hall and four reception rooms outside the enclosure. Within the enclosure there was a chapter house, cloisters, library, infirmary, community rooms, kitchen and cells for each friar, as well as this refectory. In the north-east wing, a Seraphic college (see p.14) was set up and later it was used for clergy on retreat.

The choir chapel on the first floor of the friary, 1987. The window looks out into the sanctuary of the church. The painting is of the Assumption of Our Lady and off to the left of it was a tablet to Humphrey de Trafford. He paid for this chapel, which was private for the friars, and the choir stalls were for their use. During the Second World War the friary was used by the air-raid wardens and the cellars were used as air-raid shelters.

four
Personalities

Bowling Green Gorton

Above: Young page boys sit on the steps to the sanctuary next to Father Arthur, 1960. To the left is the High altar and on the right is the base of the altar to St Anthony of Padua (see p.38). The brasses on the column (one is by Father Arthur's head) each name one of the benefactors of the monastery with the words, 'Pray for the estate of...'. Members of the Children of Mary cleaned these brasses.

Opposite above: A sketch of the monastery church, viewed from the bowling green of Gorton Park. This was drawn by George Kavanagh, an altar boy at the monastery in the early 1920s (see p.52). The original is owned by his sister, Mary Locke, the mother of Josie Faulkener, who, together with her husband Peter, has donated many items to the monastery.

Opposite below: The remaining friars in the enclosed garden by the door into the friary, in the late 1980s. Surrounding the garden were the cloisters and the friary complex. From left to right: Fathers Vincent, -?-, -?-, Gerald, Ronald the last guardian and Fabian. Usually six to ten friars were at the friary. Each had a cell (room). They did their own cooking, housework and gardening. Ladies were allowed only into the front part of the friary for mending vestments and other such activities.

The title cover for a booklet about the Franciscan order in the late 1940s, drawn by Father Basil Hodges. Once an engineer at a Tyneside shipyard and a skilled draughtsman specialising in the design and development of marine engine and steam valve gear, he was ordained as a late vocation and came to Gorton. Here he incorporates the motto of the order (see p.28) with the Latin for 'May [Christ] crucified be praised, whom he [St Francis] crucified with him praises'.

Father Basil Hodges continued his artwork for relaxation at the friary. He presented four works to Austin Fawley in 1952, who has gifted them back to the Monastery Trust. This is 'The Welder' in grey, black and white. Father Basil, who was allowed to wander around the nearby railway works of Beyer Peacock, captured this image of a man at work. The other two are a watercolour painting of the monastery church from the back and side and a sketch of a bird, made in the nearby Belle Vue zoological gardens.

The Gorton community of friars, 1961. From left to right, back row: Father Oliver, Father Arthur, Father Campion, Brother Kevin, Father Theodore, Brother Joseph, Father James, Brother Stanislaus. Front row: Father Rudolph (vicar). Father Aidan Jackson (guardian 1960-?), Father Finbar. 'I will always remember the monks going about their business along Gorton Lane in their brown habits and sandals. People passing on the bus used to stare at them.' (Pat & Bill Jackson, 1950s)

A Whit Walk in the early 1950s. The friars walk along Crossley Street with Gorton Lane behind them and Brook House flats on the right. On the left is the Co-operative store next to the tram and post office. From left to right: Fathers Walter, Arthur, Roderick O'Hagan (guardian 1948-1954), -?-, -?-, Aidan.

Above: A Whit Walk in the late 1950s. From left to right: Fathers Theodore, Arthur, -?-, Martin Crawley (guardian 1957-1960), Athanasius, Luke, Bruno, Rudolph.

Opposite above: A Whit Walk from the monastery in the late 1940s. From left to right: Fathers Roderick, Vincent, Victor, Charles Murphy (guardian 1942-48), Brother -?-.

Opposite below: A Whit Walk along Gorton Lane, May Sunday 1956. They are moving westwards towards Clowes Street, approaching the monastery. From left to right: Fathers Victor, Aidan, Edward, Bruno, Walter Hobson (guardian 1954-57), Arthur,-?-, -?-, Pacificus Tait, who was a Gorton man and later died in South Africa on missionary work. On the left, Eddie Rock holds the banner string. Behind them on the south side of Gorton Lane is a row of shops. In 1965, the shops were, from left to right: Fairfield's grocery, Travis & Groom's greengrocery, a hairdresser's shop, Miss Bruce's Catholic Repository, a private house, W. & C. Evans chemist's shop (next to Wilkes' dry cleaning business on the corner of Ritson Street).

Left: Altar boy George Kavanagh, *c.*1918. George (1909-1974) served as an altar boy when he lived at Neill Street in Gorton. He was an artist and drew the sketch of the boys' school, the original of which was kept at the friary at Forest Gate in London (see p.82). He also sketched the monastery from Gorton Park (see p.46).

Right: Altar boy Paul Griffiths aged about twelve in around 1965. Paul brought his wife Elaine to view the derelict monastery church and they went on to found the Trust, of which Paul is chairman.

The altar boys with Father Robert, 1949. From left to right, back row: Leo Allen Paul, -?-, Vincent McGrath (Father Stephen), Cyril Mannion, Ray Mannion, -?-, Mitchell, Bernard Wood. Next row: Brian Murphy, Cyril Wood, Gerald McGuire (Father Crispin), Terry King, Bernard Roddy, Brian Goodwin, -?-, John O'Brien, -?-, Tony Bush, Joe McGrath. Fourth row: third Gerald McAsey. They are outside the Parochial Hall and Brook House flats lie behind them.

The altar boys in the school yard in the 1940s. Behind them is the friary private chapel. On Sundays there were five masses at which to serve, at seven, eight, nine, ten and eleven o'clock. The congregation was so large that all these masses were needed. At the Christmas Eve midnight mass, people stood in both the side and central aisles and the doors had to be shut, as the church was filled to capacity.

The altar boys, 1945. From left to right, back row: John Travers, Hubert Travers, Billy Walker, Kenneth Goodwin, Cyril Mannion, Danny O'Brien. Next row: Brian Murphy, Bernard Wood, Joe McGrath, Arthur Nearey, Ray Mannion, Vincent McGrath. Arthur's son, Arthur C. Nearey, was baptised, married and then ordained on 21 February 1970, at the monastery church. Next row seventh from left is Bernard Roddy and front row third from left is Gerald McAsey.

The altar boys, 1964. Brother Stanislaus is on the left, Brother Gerald (Dennis) is in the centre and a visiting Swiss priest is on the right. They are at the back of the friary in front of the walkway. They wear red capes over white surplices over red cassocks: these were for special occasions.

Brother Gerald (Dennis) stands with some of the senior altar boys, 1964. The walkway is behind them. From left to right, back row: Paul O'Brien, Philip Warburton, Edmund Kenna, Charles Drainey, Michael Heffernan. Front row: Anthony Locke, Francis Berry, Patrick Colfer, Gerald Rowen, Brother Gerald. The bell-cote of the girls' school is in the background.

five

Special
Occasions

A wedding taking place in the monastery church in the 1950s. The groom and his bride stand before the High altar, just one of countless couples who were married by the Franciscan friars. Photographed from the organ loft, the view shows the High altar in all its detail with the pulpit on the left and the altar to St Anthony of Padua just visible on the right through the columns.

CERTIFIED COPY of an ENTRY OF MARRIAGE
Pursuant to the Marriage Act 1949

WARNING: A CERTIFICATE IS NOT EVIDENCE OF IDENTITY.

AA 4966

Registration District *Chorlton*

Marriage solemnized at *the Church of St Francis Gorton* in the *District* of *Chorlton* in the County of *Lancaster*

When Married.	Name and Surname.	Age.	Condition.	Rank or Profession.	Residence at the time of Marriage.	Father's Name and Surname.	Rank or Profession of Fat
Tenth May 1879	William Carroll	25 years	Bachelor	Stoker	85 Herald Street Openshaw	John Carroll	Coachman
	Bridget Egan	23 years	Spinster	—	6 Peter Street Openshaw	John Egan (deceased)	Labourer

In the *Church of St Francis* according to the Rites and Ceremonies of the *Roman Catholic Church* by *Certificate* by me *Frederick Beale*

Married: + The mark of William Carroll / + The mark of Bridget Egan
in the Presence of us, John Sidney / + The mark of Mary Egan
Joseph Jotman, Registrar

a true copy of an entry in a register in my custody,

R. Cook Superintendent Registrar 18 August 200

The wedding certificate of a couple married in the monastery church on 10 May 1879. William Carroll, aged twenty-five and born in around 1854, was a stoker from Openshaw. He was the son of a coachman, John Carroll. He married Bridget Egan, aged twenty-three, also of Openshaw. She was the daughter of the late John Egan, a labourer. William might have worked at the nearby railway works or in a close by mill or engineering works. Three of the signatures are only marks, indicating that they could not write.

D 226848

CERTIFIED COPY of an ENTRY OF MARRIAGE.
Pursuant to the Marriage Acts, 1836 to 1898.

The Statutory Fee for this Certificate is 2s. 7d. If required subsequently to registration, a Search or is payable in addition.

[Printed by authority of the Registrar-General]

Registration District **Manchester South.**

1933 Marriage Solemnized at *the Church of St Francis, Gorton* in the District of Manchester South. in the County of Manchester

No.	When Married.	Name and Surname.	Age.	Condition.	Rank or Profession.	Residence at the time of Marriage.	Father's Name and Surname.	Rank or Profession of Fat
67	Twenty fourth July 1933	Edgar William Blackshaw	24 years	Bachelor	Railway Engine Cleaner	120 Mill Street Crewe	William George Blackshaw	Engine Driver
		Evelyn Frances Kilkenny	20 years	Spinster	Milliner	152 Thomas Street Gorton	Edward Laurence Kilkenny	Clerk

Married in the *Church of St Francis* according to the Rites and Ceremonies of the *Roman Catholic* by *Certificate* by me

This Marriage was solemnized between us, E. Blackshaw / E. Kilkenny
in the Presence of us, E. Kilkenny / E. Kilkenny
Edward McGhee / H.C. Saunderson, Registrar

I, *H.C. Saunderson*, Registrar of Marriages for the District of Manchester South, in the County of Manchester, do hereby certify that this is a true copy of the Entry No. 67 in the Register Book of Marriages for the said District, and that such Register Book is now legally in my custody.

WITNESS MY HAND this 24 day of July, 1933. H.C. Saunderson

CAUTION.—Any person who (1) falsifies any of the particulars on this Certificate, or (2) uses it as true, knowing it to be false, is liable to Prosecution under the FORGERY Act, 1913.

Registrar of Marri

A wedding certificate recording a marriage in the monastery church on 24 July 1933. Edgar Blackshaw, aged twenty-four, was a railway engine cleaner from Crewe. He was son of the late William Blackshaw, an engine driver. He married Evelyn Kilkenny, aged twenty, a milliner from Gorton. She was the daughter of Edward Kilkenny, a clerk. Both Gorton Tank and Beyer Peacock's railway works lay nearby and hatting took place in many of the adjoining towns.

Above: The wedding of Jem Foy and Minnie Whelpton in the monastery church, 1937. Here they pose with their families. The Whelptons ran a funeral parlour in Gorton at 74 Wellington Street, on the corner of Banville Street.

The signing of the marriage register in the vestry (sacristy) of the monastery church, March 1959. The groom was Ken Hardicker and his bride was Betty Gainey. Father Oliver stands on the right.

Margaret and Tony Carroll pose in front of the steps outside the front entrance of the monastery church, after their wedding on 13 October 1962. Margaret's maiden name was Holmes. One of the bridesmaids watches from the doorway behind.

Opposite below: The wedding party of Don McIlroy and Pat Cunningham, February 1959. On the right stands Father Oliver. They were married in the monastery church, and are posing on the steps in front of the main entrance. Behind Don stands his brother Pat on the left and his brother Frank on the right. Bridesmaid Margery Taylor is in the front on the left.

Above: The wedding of Margaret Armstrong to Eddie Kenna on 28 September 1968. The group poses in front of the High altar, where Eddie served as head altar boy. With them are around ninety to one hundred altar boys, all arrayed in red capes over white surplices and red cassocks, which were reserved for special occasions.

Opposite above: Colin Southworth and his bride Irene (*née* Walsh) sign the marriage register in the vestry (sacristy) of the monastery church, September 1961. Colin worked as a zookeeper at Belle Vue as a young man.

The door to the sacristy was by the altar to the Sacred Heart, at the north end of the aisle (see p.39). Oak chests beneath the windows stored vestments and sacred vessels. Each friar had a place for his own things. The clock bore Crossley's name. In 1875 an iron safe from Bates of Droylsden was installed at a cost of £100

Opposite below: Hermando Fernandes signs the marriage register with his bride Pat (*née* Hodson), in the vestry of the monastery church, 1962.

A Golden Wedding blessing in the derelict monastery church on 30 March 2001. Lilian and Stan Smith were married in St Francis's church in 1951 and returned to receive this blessing on their fiftieth anniversary from Revd David Gray. Couples married in the monastery were invited back to share a special anniversary hour, including music, memories and a blessing, accompanied by the musicians from the Royal Northern College of Music

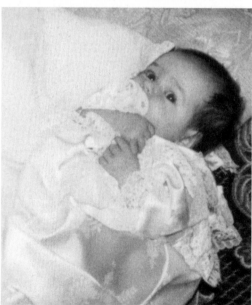

In 1891, 225 baptisms took place annually and this rose to 296 by 1899, as the number of parishioners grew. The baptismal photograph of Carla Joanne Morrissey is on the left. Baptised on 20 November 1987, Carla was one of the last babies to be christened in the monastery church. On the right is Carla Joanne Morrissey, aged fifteen in 2002.

The christening of Marianne Neill, May 1976. Held by her godparents, Thomas and Christine Hayden, she is outside the main entrance to the monastery church. Although wedding photographs were allowed inside, there seem to be no christening groups photographed inside the church.

First Holy Communion, 1948. Kevin and John Thatcher celebrate the occasion of their first Communion in the monastery church by being photographed in their Communion best clothes. First communicants came from the top infants' class, who also attended the May Queen (see chapter six).

REMEMBRANCE OF FIRST HOLY COMMUNION

Jean Riley Received First Holy Communion June 2nd 63.
and was Confirmed
Church St. Francis
City

REMEMBRANCE OF FIRST HOLY COMMUNION
John Riley
received First Holy Communion in St Francis Church
on the 12th day of June 1966
H. Noel O.F.M.

Above left: A certificate to record Jean Riley's first Holy Communion on 2 June 1963, from Father Aidan Jackson (guardian 1960–?).

Above right: Another certificate to record the same event for John Riley on 12 June 1966 from Father Noel. Both took place at the monastery church.

Right: Karen Thomas (*née* Griffiths), sister of Paul (see p.52) outside the monastery church, on the occasion of receiving her first Holy Communion on 26 July 1964, from the Bishop.

six

The May Queen

The crowning of Our Lady by the May Queen in the monastery church, May Sunday 1958. Eileen Harnay, attended by her male train bearers and four female cushion bearers, stands in front of the statue of Mary. Perched on the top of steps, Eileen would crown the statue with flowers, which were carried on the cushion. The altar of the Lady Chapel is on the left, behind the specially set up altar, and a friar kneels at the High altar on the right.

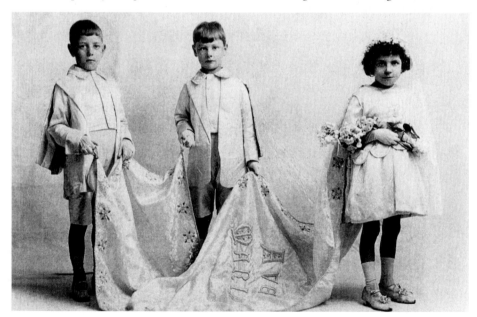

The May Queen Agnes McGuire, aged twelve, with her two train bearers posing for the camera in the late 1920s. Her long train is embroidered with the lettering, 'Ave Maria' (Hail Mary). Agnes' family had a corner shop on Gorton Lane, where she lived with her three sisters Annie, Mary and the youngest, Patsy.

Winnie McCarfre, aged seven, who was May Queen in the early 1900s. Sadly Winnie was to die at the age of eleven, knocked down by a tram near Gorton baths on Queen's Road. Apart from a gap during the war years, the May Queen ceremony would continue for many years.

The four cushion bearers and the May Queen lined up in the school yard, May 1946. Behind them on the right is the edge of the foundation stone of the school, with the monastery church to the right. The maids of honour are all dressed in their finery, ready to take part in the Whit Walk.

The May Queen with her bouquet of white lilies and preceded by her four cushion bearers, walks in front of her train bearers, in the early 1950s. Miss Holt, headmistress of the infants' school, walks alongside them, as they progress past Birch Street Baptist church, in the Whit Walk. Each year the queen was chosen from the top class in the infants' school and that class of First Communicants provided all her attendants: page boys, cushion and train bearers and maids of honour.

Above: The May Queen, taking part in a Whit Friday Walk, 1956. With her train held now by four bearers, she leads the banner of the monastery church carried by Frank Fitzgerald. Behind are her maids of honour. They are walking along Gorton Lane, away from the monastery church in the background and past Brook House flats.

Right: The May Queen, Eileen Harnay, crowning the statue of Our Lady with flowers in the monastery church, 1958. The statue is surrounded by vases of flowers, including roses and white lilies, which are both symbols of Mary and of her purity. The crowning would take place at exactly the moment in the hymn that the congregation sang the words, 'crown thee' in the chorus, 'Oh, Mary, we crown thee with blossoms today'. The crown of lily of the valley flowers again symbolises the purity and humility of Mary.

Previous pages: The May Queen, Angela Barlow, just after crowning the statue of Our Lady with flowers, 1959. The train bearers hold her discarded train. The details of the canopy and the altar are clearly visible with the words 'Ave Maria' across the base and the lettering 'Regina salve', (Queen, hail), with the badge of Mary across the top. The blue curtains bearing these words, came from the altar of the Lady Chapel and the statue itself was stored in the friary. The High altar has the placard 'altare privilegiatum' below it.

Above: The May Queen, Angela Barlow, with her four train bearers in a Whit Walk, May 1959. Alongside her walks Miss Holt, the headmistress of the infants' school. It was an honour to be chosen as queen but also an expense for her family. That year, Angela's family paid £31 13s 7d for May Sunday: the lace for her dress alone cost £5 17s 11d and the vestment brocade for her train £8.

Opposite above: The May Queen, Angela Barlow, waits with her four cushion bearers holding the cushion with its crown of flowers, in the infants' school yard, 1959. For a period of between ten to eleven years from 1959, Agnes McCreavey (*née* Shaw) made the dresses yearly for twenty-six maids of honour, four cushion bearers and the May Queen, as well as the cushion and the train. Her daughter, Bernadette, was herself a cushion bearer here in 1959.

Opposite below: The May Queen, Janice Jones, posing with her bouquet of white lilies and her four cushion bearers, May Sunday, 1960. The cushion with its crown of flowers, ready for the crowning, lies in front of her. Before the ceremony the May Queen and her attendants would process from the infants' school-yard around Crossley Street and Queen's Road and then to the monastery church.

Above: The May Queen, Mary Walker, accompanied by her train bearers and headed by her cushion bearers, makes her way up the central aisle of the monastery church, May Sunday 1962. Behind them walks Miss Holt, headmistress of the infants' school. Another head teacher, Miss Egan (see p.91), sits in front of Mary. The confessionals are visible behind the congregation, who are arrayed in their Sunday best, with the girls in white veils and dresses and the boys in bow ties and white shirts.

Opposite above: The May Queen, Janice Jones, with her four train bearers behind her, May 1960. Taking part in a Whit Walk, they are walking along Gorton Lane near Beyer Peacock and have just passed by the look-out tower for the air raid wardens. Behind them the banner of St Francis is carried by Eli, a choir member, the banner strings are held by members of the Guild of St Philomena (see pp.100-101) and the maids of honour follow.

Opposite below: The May Queen, Brenda Royle, posing with her four train bearers and the cushion for the crown of flowers, May Sunday 1961.

A line of maids of honour in a Whit Friday Walk, in the 1960s. They lead the May Queen, whose train and train bearers are visible just behind them on the left.

Boys and girls line the sanctuary steps of the monastery church during the ceremony of the crowning of Our Lady, May Sunday, in the 1960s. The May Queen and her cushion bearers are just visible on the left in the background.

The cushion bearers of the May Queen, Mary Walker, May Sunday 1962. The cushion they carry lies in between them.

Mary Walker with her attendants and maids of honour in front of the statue of Our Lady, May Sunday 1962. The High altar is off to the right. On the right lies the cushion with its crown of flowers and the candles are lit for Benediction.

Above: The attendants and maids of honour of the May Queen, Mary Walker, May Sunday 1962. They are in the sanctuary of the monastery church by the altar rails, witnessing the May Sunday crowning of the statue of Our Lady.

The cushion bearers of the May Queen, Marie Hartley, in front of the statue of Our Lady, May Sunday 1963. Outside the school window of the new infants' school, Brook House flats on Gorton Lane and preparations for the procession can be seen.

Above: The May Queen, Carol Bickerstaff, with her cushion bearers and train bearers in the infants' school, May Sunday 1965. The crown of flowers lies ready on the cushion.

Opposite below: The May Queen, Marie Hartley, May Sunday 1963. Preceded by her cushion bearers with the crown of lily-of-the-valley flowers and accompanied by her train bearers, she is waiting in the school yard for the pre-crowning procession. An altar boy, Joe McGrath, stands on the left at the back; altar boys escorted the May Queen and her retinue.

Above: The train bearers and the May Queen, Patricia White, in the infants' school, prior to the crowning, 1966.

Left: The cushion bearers of the May Queen, Patricia White, with their crown of flowers, in the infants' school, 1966.

seven

At School

The remnants of the frontage of the monastery complex, 1991. The infants' school lies on the far left beyond the monastery church. The front of the friary has gone. The girls' school is next, but the boys' school, which used the former school/chapel and old infants' school, has gone from the right. The prefab, which housed the seniors behind the girls' school, and the secondary school at the far end of the monastery gardens have also gone.

A drawing produced in 1956 by George Kavanagh (see p.52) of the monastery boys' school. On the right lies Gorton Lane and on the left the wall divides the boys' from the girls' school. The yard was for older boys with one at the back for juniors. On the right is the bell tower above the head teacher's room. The schools started in the temporary school/chapel in 1861, with Bernard Kirk as the head teacher. The boys spread into the infants' building next door in 1870. By 1954 the building was condemned and the school closed.

The girls' school buildings on Gorton Lane in the 1980s. In the distance is the petrol station, which stood where Crossley's works had been. Originally the school was mixed, using the nearby school chapel from 1861 (see p.11) but, with expansion, the girls were taught in a friary wing until 1874, when Father Polycarp set Brother Patrick to build this separate school, which opened in June 1877. In 1894 Father Edmund O'Sullivan added an extra classroom and in 1902 the small extension on the left was built.

The back of the girls' school, 1991. It was intended that this building would be modernised and converted into a junior section in 1938, but the Second World War intervened. An incendiary device landed, without causing too much damage, during the Blitz of 1940. The school was closed down in the 1970s.

The west side of the infants' school with the monastery church behind and Gorton Lane on the right, 1988. From 1866 the infants had their first separate school, built by the guardian Father Francis Verhagen, who raised over £1,000 from a bazaar at the Free Trade Hall in Manchester. This was an incredible sum for 1866. It lay west of the temporary school chapel, but, when these combined to form the boys' school, Father Aidan McCarthy had this new school built by 1893, here on the west side of the church.

The front of the infants' school, 1991. On the right lies the monastery church and in the distance is the Parochial Hall, which often served as extra school-rooms as the population grew (see p.15). At the far end of the infants' school was the nursery with its sandpit and swings. The foundation stone, which still exists, was laid in August 1892 by William Mather MP. It was described as the finest catholic school in Manchester and nicknamed the 'Drawing Room school'.

Standard V(a) of the girls' school in their school-yard, June 1926. Standards were another name for classes. The schools were the first Catholic schools in Gorton and served an ever increasing population. Some of the teachers at the girls' school were Miss Hayden (see pp.87 & 88), Miss Walker (see p.87) and Miss M. Keenan.

An infants' class in the 1920s. On the right stands Miss N. Jackson, who became head teacher of the school. Other head teachers were Miss Holt (see pp.72, 75, 108) and Miss Greenwood (see p. 87).

The girls of Standard III in their school-yard, 1921.

The same class when they were Standard II in their school-yard, 1920. Behind them on the left is the entrance porch to the girls' school.

2396

City of Manchester Education Committee.

SCHOLAR'S LEAVING SCHOOL CERTIFICATE

(For the guidance of Parents and Employers).

St Francis Girls' _____ School ___ Gorton ___

This is to Certify that Evelyn Kilkenny

of __ 152 Thomas __ Street, __ Gorton __

has reached the age fixed by law for leaving School, and is now eligible for employment.

Margaret Hayden Principal Teacher.

15. 6. 13

Date _July 22ⁿᵈ 1927_

A leaving certificate for Evelyn Kilkenny, who left the girls' school in July 1927. Her date of birth was 15 June 1913 and so Evelyn was aged fourteen and eligible to leave school to begin work. The certificate is signed by the headmistress of the senior girls, Margaret Hayden (see p.88).

Miss Greenwood, who was headmistress of the infants' school for nearly twenty years.

Miss Walker, who taught in the girls' school in the early days.

Left: Miss Margaret Hayden, who taught in the infants' school and then in the girls' school, where she became headmistress. Later she became housekeeper to Father Malone at the Holy Family church in Denton.

Right: Mr Thomas Kiernan, who taught in the boys' school for many years. Another teacher in that school in the 1930s was Mr J. Kilroy. The original head teacher of the first temporary school/chapel was Mr Bernard Kirk from 1861, with his staff, Miss Rogers and Miss Marr.

Standard VII of the boys' school in the boys' school-yard in the early 1920s. On the left is Mr Thomas Kiernan, the headmaster of the boys, and to the right is the class teacher of this leavers group who are all aged fourteen. This school had been once used as a soup kitchen for eight weeks, giving winter relief in 1893 and also during the engineers' strike of 1897. In 1913 the St Francis Old Boys' Association was formed.

Class 4 from the infants' school in 1937, the Coronation year of King George VI. Back row, extreme left: Kenneth Goodwin. The three boys on the other end of the row are, from left to right: Brien Condon, Martin Chaisty, Bernard Shaw.

The staff in the school-yard, 1938. Front, centre: Father Harold Richardson (guardian 1936-39). Back, centre: Mr McHugh, the headmaster of the boys' school throughout the 1930s and into the late 1950s. He had seen the school survive being hit by an incendiary bomb during the Blitz of 1940, in a war which saved the school from closure, after a plan in 1938 for a new seniors' school.

A boys' class in the boys' school-yard, 1942. Second row, third from left: Gerald McAsey. Standing left: the headmaster, Mr McHugh. Standing right: Mr Hughes, who taught the senior or 'big boys' in the large room of the school chapel. Some seniors were also taught in the prefab building behind the schools. On the left is the wall, dividing off the girls' school yard and behind are the school toilets.

A class of seven-year-old girls at the back of the church, 1945. From left to right, back row: third Sheila Doyle, fourth Sheila Mooney, sixth Ann Dennis, seventh Betty Gainey, eighth Eileen Roch. Among the next row: Ann Morris, Pat Hill, Ann Cafferty, Silvia Dyson, Sheila Thomson, Ann Worthington, Josie Swinburn. Among the third row: Pat Pearce, Winnifred Casey, Sheila Worthington, Pat Parks, Irene ?, Eve ?. Among the fourth row: Ann Smith, Kathleen Flanegan, fourth Sheila Hughes, Pauline Kendrick, Agnes Eearly, Renee Turner. Among the front row: Sheila Cooney, Pat Cooney, Sheila Johnson, Sheila Mills, Pat O'Brian.

Left: a sports team from the late 1940s with Mr McHugh and Mr McGahn. Front centre: Gerald McAsey.

Right: a school swimming team, the winners of the shield of the Manchester Senior Swimming Association in the 1940s. Left: Mr McHugh. Far right: teacher Mr McGahn next to Gerald McAsey. The school was renowned for sport, especially swimming, and the motto was 'Play the game'.

Left: Kate Doyle, *née* Field, standing in the back yard of a house overlooking Debdale Park in the early 1940s. She was housekeeper to Miss Egan, who progressed from infants' teacher to headmistress of the juniors' school (see p.75). Kate worked there until she was seventy. She died in 1965, aged nearly eighty-seven.

Right: Margaret O'Hara, a teacher at the monastery school in the 1950s. A testimonial from her head at St Joseph's, Victoria Park, Manchester, states she was a pupil from 1942 until 1947, reaching School Certificate standard.

Another boys' class in the school yard, 1951. The teachers are Mr McHugh, the head master since the 1940s (left) and Miss Brett, the class teacher (right). Dry rot in 1953 would soon cause the boys' school to be finally closed, dispersing the boys to Varna Street and Peacock Street schools, as well as to the Parochial Hall and to the 'Prefab'.

An architect's drawing of the proposed new secondary school, as seen from the bottom of the monastery garden, 1955. The building had a steel frame with glazed wall cladding. There was a four-storey wing with thirteen classrooms, at right angles to a combined assembly hall and gymnasium on the first floor. A small dining room was used for lunches, together with the hall, and there were library, art and craft and handicraft rooms, plus a science laboratory.

A junior class of girls in the friary gardens, 1955.

An infant class in the friary gardens, c.1953. From left to right, back row: Alan Cunningham, Brian Fitzgerald, Tommy Howes, Peter Bull, -?-, Philip Henry, Frank Perry, Gordon McLoughlin, David Jones, Tommy Donaghue, -?-. Second row: Josie Rorke, Elaine Flynn, Christine Casson, Christine ?, Maureen Marshall, Rosemary McAulay, Catherine Nolan, Theresa Hall, Christine Moran, Maureen Nixon, Rita Williams, Kathleen Meehan. Third row: Eileen Doherty, Linda Walker, Doreen ?, Catherine Ludwigson, Josie Jones, Maureen Booth, Jean Porter, Margaret Ryan, Anne Rice, Jean Mansell, Sandra Hardman. Front row: Stephen Clayton, Gordon Lewis, Brian Derbyshire, Julie Southworth, Michael McGlore, James Erskine, Peter McHugh, Raymond Worley.

Standard I walk with their teacher, Miss Brett, on a wet Whit Friday, May 1957. The new school introduced this school uniform in its early days.

Pupils from the boys' school walk along as part of a Corpus Christi procession in the 1950s. They each hold a candle. Only some are in uniform.

One of the top junior classes outside their classroom in the 'Prefabs', 1958. The teachers are Mr McCaughley (left)and Mr McHugh the headmaster (right). In 1957 the boys and girls were mixed for the first time, after having separate schools since 1862, which was almost from the start.

Members of a class of the girls' school, wearing uniform, walk in a Whit Friday Walk in the 1950s. They are just passing Birch Street Baptist chapel on the right.

A mixed class of secondary school pupils in their new school hall, set in the monastery gardens, in the 1960s. Now the only school left is the new St Francis's Roman Catholic primary on Ellenbrook Close. Back in 1897, at Queen Victoria's Diamond Jubilee, St Francis had the largest number of pupils attending from the neighbourhood: 1,400 at morning breakfast, 1,700 at the afternoon procession and 1,740 for tea in the evening.

eight

Groups and Events

The cast of *The Gondoliers* in an informal group, June 1945. Father Lawrence formed a choir but it was Father Agnellus Andrew, who took over this choir in 1933 and transformed it into a choral and operatic society, called The Greyfriars Players. Their first production in April 1938 was *The Mikado* in the Whitworth Hall. Father Agnellus was both producer and conductor. In 1939 they reprised *The Mikado* for a whole week at Belle Vue.

Members of the monastery band, 1958. From left to right, back row: A. Spencer, H. Wren, P. Mooney, N. Edwards, B. Abernethy, B. Salmon, P. Mitchell, P. Wren. Middle row: T. Regan, E. Whelan, F. Beswick, J. Winfindale, L. Cassiday, J. Edwards, K. Walker, P. Frogatt, B. Patchett. Front row: M. McMahon, H. Wren, A. Booth, Father Bruno, C. Thorpe (Drum Major), D. Fitzgerald (bandmaster), J. Emery, P. Emery, A. Regan. Front row sitting: B. Regan and J. Patchett.

The band was formed from parishioners by the bandmaster, Doug Fitzgerald. They took part in the Whit Walks, making a welcome addition to the procession on Whit Sunday, whereas previously two bands had had to be hired. In 1897, at a High Tea for 467 members of the Third Order, the band played at the Soirée.

The cast of *H M S Pinafore* on stage in October 1964. The Greyfriars Players performed this together with *Trial By Jury*. During the 1930s and '40s they had also staged concerts at Christmas for poorer people. During the war years they had toured the area, bringing their shows to the armed forces and having a break only briefly between 1941 and 1943.

The cast of *Iolanthe* on set, April 1968. From left to right, back row: fourth Frank Hughes, seventh Derek Garn. Front row: second Wilfred Hughes, fifth Harry Hughes, both early members and producers of earlier plays. In 1945 The Greyfriars Players had also staged a *Pageant of the Nativity*. They usually used the Parochial Hall but also performed at Belle Vue and at the Whitworth Hall, Openshaw.

The cast of *Patience* on set, November 1968. From left to right: sixth Josie Kavanagh, seventh Mary Clayson. Over the years The Greyfriars Players had toured over a fifty mile radius, broadcast for the BBC and raised vast amounts of money for charity. Between 1938 and 1948 they had staged 194 public performances and raised £3,000 for charity.

The young girls of the Guild of St Philomena with their banner follow the Children of Mary, whose banner is on the left, in the 1920s. When they were eighteen, ladies moved up from the Guild to the Children. They are walking westwards along Gorton Lane past the houses, which include Mansion House, which would be replaced by Brook House flats in the late 1940s. Another girls' group was the Agnesians who wore red cloaks, whereas the Children wore blue.

Left, Betty Hardicker (*née* Gainey) and right, Sheila Woods (*née* Doyle) in the school-yard of St Francis, 1952. Both aged fourteen, they were taking part in a Whit Walk as members of the Guild of St Philomena. Members wore a white dress under a pink cloak. They met on Wednesdays for social and spiritual activities and the Children of Mary met on a Thursday for the rosary, a sermon and benediction. By the end of the 1950s, boys were admitted and a youth club was formed.

A yearly collection card for parishioners, filled with advertisements for local shops, 1958. Catholics 'are earnestly requested to patronise the enterprising tradespeople who have so ably assisted in making this publication possible.' The front cover lists the names of the clergy, weekly services and organisations, such as the Legion of Mary, the Third Order of St Francis and the Girls' and Boys' Guilds. Inside there are tables for recording weekly 'door to door' and altar society collections.

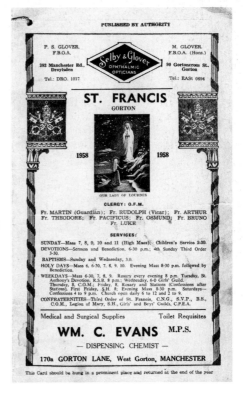

The Christmas Crib, Christmas 1951. This Nativity scene was set up each year by the altar boys and Father Gilbert near the altar of Our Lady. Painted by Frank Lloyd, it was stored in unused cells in the friary. As the kings have been added here, Epiphany must have passed.

Parishioners carrying the statue of Our Lady on a Whit Friday Walk in the 1950s. On May Sunday, the May Queen decorated the statue with a crown of flowers in the monastery church. Here the statue is surrounded with flowers that are symbolic of Mary: lilies, roses and lilies of the valley. The men usually acted as marshals for the procession.

Opposite: The Mass to celebrate the centenary of the monastery, October 1961. On Christmas Day 1861 the friars had said their first mass at Gorton in the schoolchapel, provided by Father Cardinael of Fairfield (see p.11). Here Bishop Beck is celebrating the Centenary Mass before the High altar, together with the friars acting as deacons, wearing their twin striped Dalmatic vestments.

Above: The May Queen's retinue taking part in a Whit Walk, 1938. The four cushion bearers precede the queen, Dorothy Tobin, as they walk along Gorton Lane near Peacock Street. From left to right: Helen O'Grady, Brenda Crosby, Ursula Burrows (aged six), Joyce Cunningham. Right: page boy Gerald McGuire. Brien Edward is just off the photograph.

Opposite above: Part of a Whit Walk procession, 1946. The banner of St Francis is being carried aloft by Frank Renwick, with schoolgirls holding the banner strings, followed by the young girls of the infants' school.

Opposite below: A procession for Corpus Christi in the 1950s. Members of the senior school, holding candles, are walking along Gorton Lane. Sibley Street is on the left.

Whit Walks, 1952. These young girls of the Guild of St Philomena walk along Gorton Lane. Among them, walk Betty Gainey (far right, back) and Sheila Doyle (centre, back). Sheila Doyle, both aged fourteen.

A Whit Walk returning along Gorton Lane to the monastery in the late 1950s. On the right is Jones' temperance bar, selling Vimto and Corona. In 1965 Jones' was Eaves', a herbalist. Laidlow's grocery was to the right on the corner of Evelyn Street. To the left were Willett's tobacconist's shop, then a drapery, bar and Briercliffe Street. Kathleen Mulheran walks on the left (see p.18).

Altar boys carrying the statue of Our Lady, 1952. They wore black cassocks for everyday wear, but wore red ones under white surplices for special occasions, as they do here.

On a rainy day, the banner is carried in a Whit Walk procession in the late 1950s. They are walking along Gorton Lane back to the monastery.

Above: Father Theodore waiting with young boys who are carrying candles, in a procession for Corpus Christi along Gorton Lane, 1956. The friary is in the background, fronting Gorton Lane, and the monastery church is off to the left.

Opposite above: The May Queen, Mary Walker, with her retinue, taking part in a Whit Sunday procession, 1962 (see pp.75-78). At the side of the cushion bearers walks Miss Holt, the headmistress of the infants' school and behind follows the banner of St Francis. They are passing by Brook House flats on Gorton Lane.

Opposite below: Altar boys leading the banner of St Francis along Gorton Lane, 1952. They have just passed Railway View and the railway is just off the left-hand side of the photograph. Crossley Street is the second road on the left. Terry Fitzgerald is on the left and the monastery band follows the three boys.

Above: Page boys
celebrating Corpus
Christi, processing
along Queen's Road off
Gorton Lane in the late
1940s. Terry Fitzgerald
is fourth from the right.

Right: A Whit Walk
procession in the 1960s.
The skirt lengths are
beginning to shorten
and hair styles to vary.
School pupils in uniform
walk behind with the
banner.

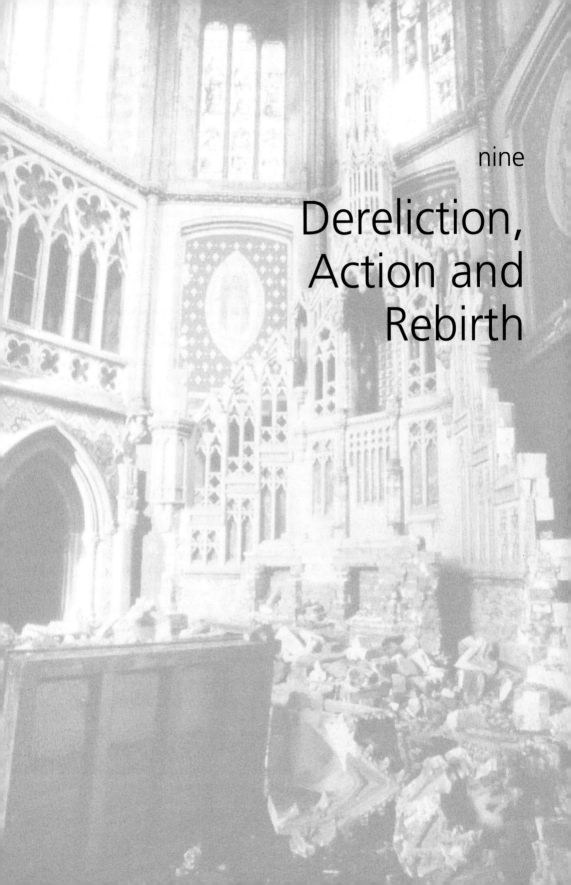

nine

Dereliction,
Action and
Rebirth

The derelict monastery viewed from the east side, 2000. On the left runs Gorton Lane. In 1989 the friars departed because, following house clearances, closure of local workplaces and a dwindling congregation, the upkeep of the huge complex was beyond the capability of the remaining guardian Father Ronald, two elderly friars and one lay brother. The last mass led by Father Ronald was attended by over five hundred parishioners at the Feast of Christ the King on 26 November 1989.

The monastery church and friary, 2000. In 1901 a new parish, the Sacred Heart, was formed in Gorton, moving some parishioners from the monastery. In the 1960s and early 1970s, with the demolition of terraced housing, the population of the parish fell from about 6,000 in 1901 to 300-400. The poor condition of the front façade of the friary resulted in its demolition in the 1970s, when this brick wall enclosed the cloister garden and the south end of the east wing on the right was sealed off with this wall.

The north or back end of the complex, 2000. In 1980, the guardian Father Vincent had appealed for £100,000 for new heating, reroofing and removal of dry rot. He received £64,000 from English Heritage to reroof the church and for exterior repairs. This probably saved the church later. The friars left, having sold the site to a property developer, who stripped out the church to convert it into eighty-four flats (see p.118). In 1993 the scheme failed and the site lay open to vandals and thieves.

The city council eventually made the building waterproof in 1994. But by then, inside, the nave had been stripped of its seating and the sanctuary of its treasures. All that could be reached had been taken, including the lead from the friary roof and the 8ft high sandstone statues.

These are the remains of the High altar standing amidst its own rubble and destruction, 2000. The lofty height of the church saved features too high up, such as the wall paintings of the archangels, the stained glass windows and the stone carvings on the walls and the top of the reredos. The Grade II monastery complex was actually upgraded to Grade II★ during this traumatic period.

Above: A wall of the monastery church, damp with peeling plaster, with the plinths vacant of their saints, but with the angels below them still in situ (see p.116). The empty church became a campsite for travellers and was later occupied by Friends of the Earth, anxious to protect what was left. In September 1996, the Monastery of St Francis & Gorton Trust was formed by volunteers, as a building preservation trust to save the monastery complex. By December 1996, charitable status was granted.

Right: The altar of the Lady chapel was robbed and vandalised. The other three side altars suffered a similar fate, with that of the Blessed John Forest almost totally removed. In September 1997 the monastery was first placed on the World Monuments Fund Watch List of the 100 most endangered sites, alongside the Taj Mahal, Pompeii and the Valley of the Kings.

Left: Here an angel survives below the carved plinth where its saint had once stood. The wall shows the ravages of damp and exposure to the weather from broken windows. In October 1997 the Royal Bank of Scotland sold the complex to the Trust for a token £1 and so grant fundraising could begin.

Below: Some of the twelve statues of the saints removed from the monastery church. These 6ft-high sandstone statues resurfaced in a 1994 auction catalogue at Sotheby's, with a reserve price of £2,000 each. Their fate was to be sold as garden ornaments to American customers but, through the diligence of a local resident, Janet Wallwork, they were saved. From left to right: St Anthony of Padua, St Leonard of Port Maurice, St Louis of Toulouse, St Berard, St Clare, St Louis of France and St Ivo.

Right: The statues in their secret storage location, awaiting restoration and a return to the monastery church. From left to right: St Clare and St Louis of France. Manchester City Council saved the saints by paying £25,000 for them to be taken out of the auction and to go into storage.

Below: A violinist, New Zealander Juliette Primrose, in the cloisters, 2003. The cloisters enclosed the four sides of the inner garden of the friary and connected the different parts of the friary and also the church to the friary complex. Juliette played a solo to mark the visit of the Duke of Gloucester to the monastery (see p.127).

Left: A staircase leading down in the friary to the cloisters and via the door to the monastery enclosed garden. These stairs led to the friary's private chapel on the first floor and connected the three-storey wing with the rest of the friary. The Gothic-style cloisters were each 100ft long with plain arches and a simple, tiled floor.

Below: The cover of the developer's glossy brochure advertising the proposed development of eighty-four flats, 'St Francis Cloisters', 1990. The Nottingham-based company promised a beautiful conversion 'to outstanding luxury apartments'. An on-site leisure centre with gymnasium, saunas and solariums was to bring 'a lifestyle experience combining the best of the new and the old'. Each flat was to have a well-equipped kitchen and bathroom and a choice of fitted carpets. The grounds were to be landscaped and have a fountain. The developers had agreed to keep the High altar and stained-glass windows but they stripped the building of many of its features, leaving it open to theft and vandalism.

ST. FRANCIS CLOISTERS

An inspection of the exterior of the monastery church. During 1997 and 1998, a feasibility study was carried out to assess the best use of the building. Here the 'cherry-picker' hoist even allowed inspection of the Calvary on the front of the monastery church, almost 100ft off the ground. In 1998 the 'Spirit of Life' plan was unveiled for the friary as 'a common experience from birth to death and beyond' and for the garden and church to host exhibitions, conferences and concerts. However, the idea failed to attract funding.

The inspection of the nave near the sanctuary of the monastery church, as part of the feasibility study. The 'cherry-picker' hoist allowed access to the very ceiling of the church, even though it is nearly 90ft high. In December 1997, Christopher Charles Dickens, the great-great-grandson of the novelist, became patron of the Trust. On his death in 1999, the Trust benefited from the sale of his Dickens archive.

The first of many open days held by the Trust, Heritage weekend September 1998. The monastery has been opened up for weekends and special events to allow both local people and former parishioners access to the buildings. Entrance has been through the gate into the friary garden, along the cloisters into the church. Occasionally the front doors have also been opened up. Several thousand visitors turned up for the first opening and queued from the cloisters out onto Gorton Lane.

Right: One of the open days at the monastery church. Local and heritage groups have put on displays and workshops, and the Trust sells souvenirs and exhibits future plans and results of action taken. A blank board allowed memories to be recorded and emotions described. An archive of photographs and memorabilia for the monastery and for the local area was established.

Below: An open day. The front doors are open, letting light flood into the nave of the monastery church. The bare floor, empty building and stripped walls possess their own dignity, as the pigeons fly around and people gaze in awe at the size and height of the empty building, resembling a cathedral in scale. Open topped buses from the Manchester Museum of Transport ferried visitors between the museum and the monastery. In 1999, 5,000 visitors attended.

Another open day with displays set around the edges of the walls and by the columns of the nave. On the High altar the lit candles add to the light in the darkened church. In 2000, plans for a hotel were proposed for Heritage Lottery funding. The friary would house seventy Franciscan style bedrooms, with the church acting as a conference, events and meeting venue. Sadly, following the events of 11 September 2001, the hotel scheme became unfeasible.

The west wall of the church with its confessionals on an open day. The empty plinths are above the columns, where saints stood, with the angels still at their feet. A book of Inspiration was compiled from the thoughts, prayers, wishes and memories recorded on the board in the Lady chapel. In 2000, Terry Waite agreed to become patron of the Trust, replacing the late Christopher Charles Dickens.

Left: Another open day with the High altar as a backdrop for an East European dance group called Opanka. Children's choirs, Gorton symphony orchestra, dancing displays and music groups all participated in the events and celebratory services.

Below: The Stockport Barbershop choir entertain in the church, 2001. Many groups and individuals have given freely of their time to sing, dance, play music or entertain on open days and at special events.

Amici Choir, 2001. Events and simple services have been held in the ruins of the church. The Manchester Adventist gospel choir participated in the Carols by Candlelight concert on 3 December 2000 and celebration services have been held at the end of each open weekend and at Easter Sunday. The Trust also participates in, and helped to initiate, an annual Gorton Festival.

Members of the 'Friends of the Monastery Trust', 2003. From left to right, back row: John Griffiths, Brian Currie, Margaret Jones, David Ratcliffe, Claire Woody, Frank Rhodes, Diane Mercer-Brown, Paul Farrell, Graham North. Middle row: Kath North, Vera Bromage, Janet Wallwork, Audrey Bradshaw, Revd David Gray. Front row: Megan Neesom, Peter Koudellas, Marie Koudellas, Florence Wallwork.

The banqueting scene from Shakespeare's *Macbeth*, which was filmed by Granada Television Productions at the monastery for Channel 4 in 1999. The hiring of the monastery church at various times has helped to generate funds and publicise the needs of the site. Over the past eight years, since 1996, the small band of volunteers, who manned the first open day which was swamped by visitors, has grown into a vast network of 'Friends', who bring their many skills to help the project.

Left: In 2002 the plans for a Pugin centre received Heritage Lottery funding. The centre was to incorporate museums for Pugin, East Manchester (itself including Belle Vue), and the Story of St Francis. In July 2002, the monastery was open as a 'Hall of Heritage' during the fortnight that the Commonwealth Games took place nearby. On 26 July, Terry Waite, as patron, announced the funding success in the monastery church.

Below: A special reception at the monastery church, 2 August 2002. From left to right: the Lord Mayor of Manchester, the Rt Hon. Gerald Kaufman MP, Arlene McCarthy MEP, Elaine Griffiths (Project Director). They are celebrating the success of the Heritage Lottery funding bid. On the closing of the Commonwealth Games, a service was held in the church. The plans include 'An Angels Community Village' for healthy living and restoration of the private chapel of the friary and of the High altar itself.

The visit by the Duke of Gloucester to the monastery, 3 April 2003. This boosted the campaign to save the monastery. Left: the Duke of Gloucester. Right: Elaine Griffiths (Project Director). A scheme was launched, called 'Save A Saint and Adopt An Angel', whereby a Certificate of Support and a replica angel are received for sponsoring one of the choir of angels, to fund restoration of the stonework.

Left and below: Two images of the young stonemasons at work mark the rebirth of the monastery complex. Workshops have been run for school groups and young people to be involved in learning stonemasonry, which is one of the many skills needed in the restoration of the monastery. Visitors during the restoration will view the craftsmen at work and watch the project develop.

This is not the end but just the beginning of restoration and renewal.

HIGH ALTAR.
FRANCISCAN CHURCH WEST CORTON.

The original plan for the altar and reredos *c.* 1894. This lithograph made for the reredos was designed by Peter Paul Pugin, the half-brother of E.W. Pugin who designed the monastery. When finished it was almost exactly as this plan. Despite the current dereliction, the altar has a tragic beauty all of its own, and should perhaps be left unrestored as a poignant reminder of what has happened here.

ten

Restoration

Before any of the restoration work on the buildings could begin, the grounds had to be cleared of all of the overgrowth and the rubbish that had accumulated over the years. In this picture we can see the first stage of the clearance, with the aid of a JCB to pull out the bushes and weeds.

The full extent of the dereliction can be seen in this picture on the left, which shows a doorway into a ground floor room in the friary. The two upper floors have collapsed right through to the cellars. This is mainly because the slate roof tiles had been removed soon after the monastery closed leaving the friary exposed to successive bad winter weather.

This is the main stairway in the friary. It is covered in debris from the walls and the ceilings as the work on the restoration was gaining momentum. The whole stairway was completely gutted and replaced with a new staircase. This picture was taken on the 14 January 2006.

The picture below, taken on the same day, shows more of the debris in the friary, this time on the ground floor. This is where the original kitchen stood. During the restoration the tiles were all removed and replaced with plaster, and the window frames were replaced with frames that reflected the original windows.

Left: The cloisters, 28 May 2006. The floor is littered by beams and rubble from above. At the end of this corridor there used to be a stairway, which had suffered extensive fire damage due to vandalism. The stairs will eventually be rebuilt in a new housing to the left, and the end of this corridor will be the main entrance.

Bottom: All of the walls have been tested in various places and it has been decided that the structure is sound so the restoration work continues as the friary walls are completely covered in scaffolding. By the time this picture was taken on 26 June 2006 the three topmost courses of bricks have been replaced in readiness for the new roof.

Above: By August 8th 2006, the friary roof had been rebuilt. Here the tiles have been laid out ready for nailing in place. The chimneys have all been re-pointed and soon the new roof will be completed.

Left: A busy view showing what will become the new main entrance to the monastery, 26 April 2006. The walls have been stripped of the render and here you can see the original (large) archway on the right, which formed part of the first chapel on this site, *c.* 1863. This is the chapel that was in use while the main monastery was being built.
The two visible doorways high up in the wall show that there have been numerous alterations to the plan of the buildings.

This picture, taken on the 24 April 2006, shows a man working on one of the chimneys on the roof of the friary, preparing the brickwork ready for the new roof to be installed. On the chimney you can see the line where the roof was and the dark stain is from years of being exposed to the weather, and industrial smoke.

When the front of the friary was demolished, this wall had been bricked over and a large mirrored Franciscan cross placed on the outside, This photo reveals the original archway in the cloisters. The cloisters continued around what is now the garden wall. The area to the right of the arch now houses the new lift and staircase. The arch is now the main entrance to the monastery.

Right: On Valentine's Day 2004 a film production company, Music Zone, screened *Romeo and Juliet* starring Leonardo de Caprio. It was on a freezing winter evening, but the low temperature did not dampen the audiences' enthusiasm, as everybody who attended thoroughly enjoyed the show. These dancers were part of the entertainment.

The BBC filmed the Gorton Voice Choir in the monastery for one of their *Songs of Praise* programmes. This picture, taken on the 25 March 2007, shows the extent of the scaffolding inside the building. In the background you can see the crucifix, returned the previous November, and the choir standing by ready to sing. The camera crew with their long boom camera are situated below a large gantry placed high above to help steady the scaffolding.

An aerial view of the monastery, taken as part of the preparations for the visit of HRH The Prince of Wales and The Duchess of Cornwall on 7 February 2007. At this time the entire monastery was covered top to bottom in scaffolding, both inside and outside the buildings. Here, the roof of the friary has been completely rebuilt and all of the windows are in the process of being replaced, the spire is being cleaned and repointed and the church roof checked for any damp.

The workmen in this picture are working at the rear end of the church. They work for the contractors William Anelay and Son Ltd, and they all seem to be enjoying their work. Most of the restoration work was carried out by William Anelay and Son Ltd who have a vast amount of experience in this kind of restoration work

This picture, taken from the scaffolding erected when the stained glass windows were being restored, shows the view towards the front of the church. The workmen closest are involved in re-installing the windows at the sides of the sanctuary. The church floor has been strengthened and the next job will be to clean and repaint the walls. When all the scaffolding has been removed the new under-floor heating will be installed.

The roof of the cloisters had to be removed along with the rotting plaster from the walls. The walls will be faced with new lime plaster and specially imported Welsh slate tiles will form the new roof. The leaded windows will be replaced, and the floor tiles will be renewed where they cannot be repaired.

An interesting feature in the cloisters is the apse, which again had its roof and plaster removed and replaced, and is now awaiting restoration to its former splendour.

On the 2 November 2006 the crucifix came back to its rightful place in the monastery after more than 15 years away. The cross, crafted 130 years ago by Father Cuthbert Wood out of reconstituted stone, was about to be sold at auction by art dealer Patricia Wengraf, until the Monastery Trust managed to secure its return for a much reduced £20,000.

Among many other items to be returned have been the original blueprints for the monastery schools, a small bell, and various other plans for the original monastery buildings.

The original statues of the Calvary have also been returned from an army chapel, all in very good condition although the wooden cross had been replaced with a new one.

This statue of the Madonna and Child has been returned to the monastery in excellent condition, by Gladys and Frank Rhodes whose son, Paul, had bought it in the late 1990s.

Also returned was this rosary (below) which had been given to Mr Michael Rhodes, no relation, by Brother Gerard well before the monastery was closed.

During the restoration a large hoarding was erected along Gorton Lane. This was decorated with a large time line with the history of Gorton and the monastery running along the bottom. Here we can see people reading the timeline during the unveiling. The hoardings were reproduced on rolls of vinyl and given out to schools in the area for educational purposes, and also printed in book form which were for sale to the public.

These men, pictured on the 28 September 2006, are installing the new windows high up on the wall of the church, above the western side of the High Altar. These plain glass windows had to be completely replaced, while the stained glass windows behind the Altar were largely intact and so have been restored rather than replaced.

The first phase of the restoration is nearly complete. Here we can see the under-floor heating system has been installed and a layer of cement is being laid on top. The cement took six months to settle properly after which the new flooring was laid.

When the original flooring was removed in the 1960s, it was replaced with modern marble tiles, donated by the Quilligotti family. By the time the restoration began they had deteriorated to such an extent that the floor had to be replaced. This was the perfect opportunity to install under-floor heating. Here we can see where the piping was fed through to the heating system. The pipes were laid onto thick polystyrene and then cemented over.

Setting the paving stones in the friary garden. Here we can see some students from Mancat, now Manchester College, laying the paths in the friary garden on 9 April 2008. The garden has been designed in keeping with the style of the original plan from the time that the friars used to keep the garden. The trees have survived from before the closure of the monastery.

The friary garden in June 2008. The cobbled paths, laid by students from Manchester College, with help from the probation services, and the new lawns combine to make this a peaceful place to sit and rest. The garden has now been named The Cloister Garden.

eleven

Renaissance

HRH The Prince of Wales and The Duchess of Cornwall visiting the monastery, 7 February 2007. At that time there were no windows in the building and although the sun was shining, it was a very cold day. Even so, they enjoyed their visit, and stayed much longer than we had expected them to. Here they are seen walking through the cloisters, and below, Prince Charles bids farewell to Trust Chairman Paul Griffiths following a most enjoyable visit. Behind the Prince you can see Mr Terry Waite who is a patron of the monastery.

A midsummer nights feast, 21 June 2007. This was the first banquet held in the monastery following the restoration and the guests were treated to a fine dinner. At the far end you can see the carving of the ox, which had been roasted in the friary garden during the afternoon. The guests included many prominent businessmen.

A large number of models from the Boss Model Agency line up at the end of a fashion show, as another group enters the cat walk. This event on the 5 July 2007, was one of the first large events held in the monastery since its re-opening and it was a great success.

Left: Aled Jones' first visit to the monastery, 2005. He was appearing in the first BBC *Songs of Praise* programme to feature the monastery. Here he is singing *Be still for the presence of the Lord*. He sang the same song in 2008, and the two recordings were merged together for the finale of the second *Songs of Praise* programme which was broadcast in 2008.

In February 2008 the BBC and Aled Jones returned to the monastery to film two shows, *Songs of Praise: Young Choir of the Year*, and a second *Songs of Praise* telling the story of the restoration of the monastery. The filming took four days to complete and the programmes were broadcast during the summer of that year.

The Gorton Philharmonic Orchestra performing their first concert to a full house in the monastery, 14 July 2007. They returned in 2008 with a performance of Gustav Holst's *Planet Suite* in its entirety, which again attracted another full house.

The Gorton Philharmonic Orchestra played another concert on 12 July 2009. Pictured here, from left to right are: Conductor Nicholas Simpson, Janet Wallwork Gorton Monastery Trustee, Lord Mayor's Consort Andrew Fox, The Lord Mayor of Manchester Councillor Alison Firth, John Boydell Secretary of the Orchestra, and Elaine Griffiths, Chief Executive of the Gorton Monastery Trust.

This concert in the monastery on 10 October 2007 starred internationally famous tenor Martin Toal, and violinist Craig Owen. Their performances were so popular that they have both returned to peform in other concerts.

A concert by the St Georges Singers, 20 September 2007. Two of their Patrons are Terry Waite and Dame Joan Bakewell, who are also Patrons of Gorton Monastery. They can be seen here sitting at the front, centre left. The St Georges Singers returned to perform in the monastery in 2008 and 2009.

A single table set for 18 places in the private chapel, on the first floor of the friary. This room with its large stained glass windows was originally used by the friars as their private chapel. Now it is used mainly for small, intimate dinners, but it can also be booked for small wedding parties and naming ceremonies.

A large array of clergy from all different denominations lined up alongside the Spirit of Love sculpture at its unveiling, 30th August 2007. The sculpture, dedicated to Mother Theresa, was commissioned by Mr Osman Caka, whose son Ilir was murdered in Kosova. Sculpted in white stone by Andrew Scantlebury, it stands outside the front of the monastery.

Guests from around the world attended The Discovery Gala Dinner hosted by Visit Britain, with the theme *The Mad Hatter's Tea Party*, 21 October 2008. Here we can see the Mad Hatter, a bird and the March Hare. There were also jugglers, a dormouse, the Queen of Hearts and her pack, a spectacular trapeze act, Alice plus other characters from the Lewis Carroll stories.

Young, Gifted and Green performing at the monastery, 9 March 2009. The students are from St Bedes College, Levenshulme, and they are performing routines from the show *Riverdance*. The entertainment also included young Irish musicians, singers, and a choir of young children who sang traditional Irish songs.

A knight on horseback, a jester, a fool and a juggler were the entertainment for a medieval banquet held in the monastery, 11 July 2009. There were also two minstrels who played incidental music throughout the evening.

twelve

The Future

A large audience for a Diane Cooper Spiritual Awareness Day at the monastery,12 October 2008. The event included speeches, meditation, singing, with stalls in the cloisters and the main space. During the lunch break people enjoyed the sunshine in the cloister garden.

A regular feature of the Sunday open days in the monastery is this labyrinth. It is printed on large sheets of canvas, and is laid across the floor in the main space. Many visitors walk the labyrinth to experience its calming qualities. It is a full size replica of the labyrinth at Chartres Cathedral.

Anyone wishing to visit the monastery and learn about its history can now book a tour. They are usually conducted by the monastery historian, Mr Tony Hurley, and include information about the history of the Franciscans in Britain, the building of the monastery, its sacred geometry and its purpose. Here he is discussing the twelve saint statues which were placed on plinths above the columns.

Almost 20 years after the closure of Gorton Monastery, the wheel has turned full circle. The monastery has succeeded in overcoming the difficulties to obtain a licence to perform wedding ceremonies again. The wedding of Emma Kelly and Daniel Karen on 27 June 2009 was the first wedding in the monastery since it reopened. In the picture below they can be seen sitting on elaborately-styled chairs ready to sign the marriage register.

The happy couple are showered with confetti as they enter the cloister garden.

Below: Emma and Daniel are photographed outside the monastery with an impressive line up of vintage wedding cars in the background.

The third wedding in the monastery since the restoration was completed, 8 August 2009. Chris and Louise, the happy couple, had long wanted to marry at the monastery, and had been instrumental in helping the monastery gain the license to conduct marriages again.

Here they are seen making their vows with the registrar, and below, in the cloister garden after the ceremony with their son Jack.

Chief Executive Elaine Griffiths was awarded an MBE for 'Services to Heritage' in the Queen's Birthday Honours List, June 2007.

Below: The monastery wins 'Project of the Year' and 'Best Conservative Project' in the North West RICS Awards, May 2009

If you are interested in purchasing other books published by The History Press, or in case you have difficulty finding any of our books in your local bookshop, you can also place orders directly through our website:
www.thehistorypress.co.uk